D1716949

For my mom
who inspired this story.

It was the night
before Christmas

and all through
the house

no creatures
were stirring

except one little
mouse!

His name was Marcus

with big eyes so bright

and fur soft and gray

his nose black as the night.

TOO excited to
sleep

so he snuck out
of bed

and crept to the
hearth

to wait for Santa
instead.

He just HAD to meet him!

He knew Santa was nice

and brought presents to children

and to good little mice.

But soon Marcus
grew sleepy,

"I'll miss him!" he
feared

when all of a sudden

SANTA appeared!

Lights on the
mantle

allowed Marcus to
see

Santa filling each
stocking

as full as can be.

Santa noticed the
young mouse

and exclaimed with
great joy-

"It's a pleasure to
meet you,

Marcus, my boy!"

"Santa!" grinned Marcus

"Those stockings look great,

but I can ADD something

to make them first rate!"

"Add something?"cried Santa

"I must disagree!

I'm the EXPERT at Christmas

No one can beat me!"

"I bet I can do it."

The determined mouse
said.

Santa smiled and
laughed,

"Be my guest! Go
ahead!"

"I'll bring you a year's worth

of cheese if you can

add anything else

to THESE stockings, young man!"

So as quick as a
mouse-

(because that's what
he was!)

Marcus nibbled a hole

in each stocking, then
paused....

"There you are,
Santa!"

Marcus said with a
wink-

"I added a hole to
them,

what do you think?!"

Well, Santa smiled and chuckled-

he knew Marcus was right!

And their friendship began

on that very night.

Every Christmas Eve now

the friends meet for dinner

and Santa brings cheese

to honor the winner.

So, whenever YOUR
socks

get a hole just
remember

how Marcus met Santa

that night in
December.

About the author:

Sue Luke is a retired pharmacist and lives in Alexandria, Minnesota with her husband, Joe, and their dog Louis. She thanks her family for their encouragement with this project!

Purebooks

"Blessed are the pure in heart for they shall see God."
Matthew 5:8

This book was published by Purebooks Publishing Company which is a part of Kelly's Complete Digital Design.

KELLYAULNOVELS.COM

Made in the USA
Monee, IL
19 October 2024

68225718R00024